QUIETLY FALLING APART

QUIETLY FALLING APART
AN INTIMATE SELECTION OF POEMS

MARK R. G.

For all the people feeling alone, struggling to find their place in the world.

You're not alone.

INTRODUCTION

This selection covers a diverse range of themes and topics, including love, loss, sadness, humour, loneliness and self-realisation. There is truly something for everyone.

The order of this selection is chronological, the first poem, *"One Question"* was written in 2012 and, the final poem, *"Prevalence Revealed"* written in 2019. The reason for this ordering is to retain the feel of a rollercoaster ride through the author's mind in a similar disorganised, chaotic way. Turning a page can take you from one emotional extreme to another.

Be prepared for laughs, shock, feels and horror on an unfiltered journey into the life of Mark R. G.

This selection holds 68 poems.

ABOUT THE AUTHOR

Mark R. G is an unknown author, debuting his intimate selection of poems to the world for the very first time. The poems contained within this selection have accumulated over many years, most of which, was written through times of high emotion and painful life experiences.

He's just a human who opened up to the pages with his words when he feared ears would not understand them.

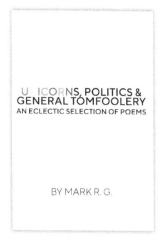

UNICORNS, POLITICS &
GENERAL TOMFOOLERY
AN ECLECTIC SELECTION OF POEMS

BY MARK R. G.

Available on Amazon
Mark R. G. can be found on
Instagram | Twitter | Facebook
@MarkRGPoetry

CONTENTS

One Question

I was happy, once upon a time,
Then this curse hit me, like a victim of crime,
It happened so fast, without much thought,
To deal with this, I was not taught.

Why me! Why now, I ask sincerely,
Broken to nothing, I see not clearly,
Easing the pain, I can't help me,
When all I know is, I can't feel thee.

Now I'm empty, with one question left,
What do I do, I won't accept death?
I'll fight for my life, with my friends by my side,
Damn you Death! I'm not going to hide.

Here is the time to choose my choice,
Recover well and use my voice,
Break the curse and divide my mind,
Goodbye, Death, I choose life.

The Thought I Forgot

For what I know, I do not believe,
I'm talking of thoughts, I chose not to conceive,
They struck me, with such speed,
Be gone with these thoughts I do not need.

It's not just thoughts, but feelings too,
They come as a duo, with pain in lieu,
Hurt aplenty, suffering a must,
Why O why pick me! It's blindly unjust.

Although you can't see, my mental nightmare,
It doesn't mean its existence isn't there,
Attacking at full force, without any help,
I find no strength, no breathe for a yelp.

Low on life, beat down by my mind,
I look at the past, seeing all that was kind,
I'm better than this, rose-tinted it's not,
I can be happy, it's just a thought I forgot.

Been Long

It hasn't been long,
Since I met you,
I'd wished it been sooner,
But back then, I had no clue.

Now in my life,
here you are,
So beautifully wonderful,
More so, than the brightest star.

You make my heart race,
Every second, of every day,
Just with the thought of you,
A smile is put upon my face.

I hope with every part of me,
I can give you all and more,
And last but not least to say,
Our love will conquer all.

Ocean Divide

I wish right now,
To be by your side,
While in another country,
With an ocean divide.

I'd meet your lips,
With a kiss from mine,
Telling you with haste,
All will be fine.

Seeing you smile,
Hearing you speak,
You make my heart race,
And knees that weak.

Today is your day,
You need not fear,
For you will do great,
Stay positive, my dear.

Nothing Wrong (Included)

Nothing wrong,
Never a frown,
Until the moment,
You put me down.

It was unreal,
For the most part,
Even the dagger,
Half hinged through my heart.

Now I see,
It was a lie,
You broke me,
But I'll not cry.

Time was taken,
To get here,
Alone at the start,
An end, we all fear.

Nothing Wrong (Excluded)

Nothing wrong,
Never a frown,
Until the moment,
You put it down.

It was unreal,
For the most part,
Even the dagger,
Half hinged through the heart.

Now to see,
It was a lie,
You broke it,
But It'll not cry.

Just a nothing,
Is what you'd be,
Which is why this poem,
Doesn't contain me.

Despair, Are You There?

While in the darkness,
With no light to share,
A name is whispered,
I'm yours, I'm Despair.

It's cold and uncaring,
What a place to be,
Constantly questioning,
Why now! Why me!

To find the light,
Is to fight in the dark,
Through all the pain,
Cleansing despairs mark.

A fight is settled,
We suppress despair,
To gain strength in darkness,
Until next time, one mind, we share.

Selfish SOB

It's all about me,
Your feelings, your thoughts,
All that you are,
I live for these taunts.

Your words match silence,
Unless they're of me,
Your eyes mean nothing,
Until it's me, they see.

Live for my life,
You'll make me happy,
For as long as I keep you,
Or until you get too sappy.

This speaks for them,
Those who hurt without thought,
The selfish ones,
No compassion, they were taught.

Hello Judgement

You're here,
Not said,
Most of the time,
A thought for the head.

Depicting,
Impacting,
Another's thought,
We need not extracting.

The horror,
Those looks,
Not written,
In any books.

A mirror,
A friend,
Their honesty,
Means more in the end.

The Unicorn

She had hands of Ice,
And a heart of gold,
With just one smile,
You'll never feel cold.

The rarest of a kind,
With care so deep,
Worth all of the time,
One you'll want to keep.

No end of laughter,
Surreal to find,
In any world,
She'd be one of a kind.

A beauty of no words,
With emotions all true,
Even with her past hurt,
She would still, endlessly, love you.

Haunting

A long time ago,

When we were one,

Our time spent happy,

But now, it's long gone.

The thoughts are still left,

Of you and I,

The occasional reminder,

Of times gone by.

Now you're just a thought,

Haunting the mind,

Settled in the campus,

Thoughts of your unkind.

To eventually forget,

A point to aim for,

With the last memory to go,

The moment you closed the door.

Basic Bitch

She was false in the brow,
With a bun like the rest,
She'd dine at MacDonald's,
A basic bitch, it's how she'd dress.

Popular in school,
A truant she was,
Down in the subway,
five quid, for a nosh[1].

Thick as a plank,
A dosser by day,
Tell her of benefits,
O shit, there's a baby on the way.

It's a girl,
Not a dad in sight,
Magenta sequins her name,
The next gens fucked, that's the real fright.

---

[1] Nosh - to perform fellatio. UK slang.

Wherefore Art Thou Fuck Boy?

Jeans of tight black, with rips in the knees,
A bulge so small, it'll be hard to please,
Talking down to girls, like you the man,
When all you really are, is shit without a plan.

Treating them mean like it's the only choice,
Putting them down, with a meaningless voice,
Taking their love, with nothing to return,
Leading them on, they'll never learn.

Playing the girls, there's an endless supply,
Who wait patiently, for the right guy,
Dreaming he's out there, hoping for years,
Then she sees you, with the lads having beers.

She's the new game, getting her into bed,
When all she really wants, is a man to wed,
She ends up with you, a fuck boy you are,
Leaving her unwanted, giving her another scar.

Carbon Copy Psycho

Pierced in the nose,
Fake in the tit,
Counts burns at the gym,
Can't work a fit bit.

Generically posed,
Insta filters a mass,
Likes the fuck boys,
Who just want her ass.

Listens to Kanye,
Dresses like Kim,
A trend-following monkey,
Her personality ultra-dim.

Looking for love,
She'll never find,
Simple she is,
But a psycho in her mind.

Short Cut Short

You ask yourself,
What did I do,
Constantly wondering,
But yet, not a clue.

What did I say,
Repeating all said,
Not a single word wrong,
Or intentions misled.

Small remnants of you,
Your perfume, in the car,
A stray hair from the head,
I still find in my bed.

All I feel is guilt now,
I would have given my all,
I'd wish I'd met you sooner,
Instead of suffering in mid-fall.

Aftermath

All food without taste, alone I eat,
While replaying the time of our first meet,
The memories created, now sad and tainted,
The future just blurred, our portrait unpainted.

All smells dull, unless of their scent,
Before the ending, we were always content,
It came out of nowhere, unjustly given,
Heartlessly worded and for us, I'd always striven.

Our Foundations crumbled, down the built goes,
The mind in overdrive, from words of precise blows,
Overwhelmed with feeling, yet internally hollow,
My self-pity intact, allowing for my wallow.

The rawest moments, those days after it's done,
What will become of me, for in this I have not won,
The currency of time, waning away with each day,
Loneliness my rebound, more time to you, I'll have to pay.

Darkness Is Not Your Friend

You say to yourself,
Hey darkness, my friend,
Like it exists,
It's there, you pretend.

It's not your friend,
It's the absence of light,
You need not indulge it,
Just fight your own fight.

Taking comfort in an absence,
Is not a forward move,
You're hindering yourself inside,
Setting yourself up to lose.

Get over your fear,
Embrace in the light,
Never give up,
You're alive, that's all you need to fight.

The Perpetual Mind

Today I died, well mentally so,
All cognition but stopped, not a thought to show,
Not even a crave, no grave I need,
Not physically dead, the heads lost without heed.

Not a neuron shot, for a smile or frown,
Capsized in mind, not backwards, forwards or upside down,
We are but here again, a head storm before the calm,
Without drawn blood to be seen, a dead mind shows no harm.

When a mind is apart, the purest despair is back,
Like the first moment before life, there was no mind to crack,
You feel the awakening, as thoughts approach the mind,
The flood gates opening, all thought refilled for a bout of unkind.

Gone is the mental break, it's untoward in life,
So, we continue steadily, with the rhythm of our heart,
With every breathe, beat and thought, the minds reborn again,
Like a phoenix from the ashes we rise, until the next time, amen.

Disposable Generation

Throw away people,
What an era to be alive,
Used for a moment,
Disposed of in five.

Time is our currency,
Never refunded back,
It's given so freely,
Always keep track.

Waste it with the trusted,
Not with those who matter,
Yes, that read right,
We never choose the latter.

Life will eventually end,
Was it lived right,
Differently, we'd choose,
If we had hindsight.

All is Nothing

Edibles without taste,
No hunger for food,
Alcohol a crave,
For dulling the mood.

All enjoyment forgotten,
Nights of sleep escaping,
Running on empty,
The mind is reshaping.

Parts have torn away,
That built over time,
Feelings diminished,
In this heart crime.

The lessons the same,
Always be wary,
Trusting in anyone,
Will always be scary.

Rinsed Heart

Heartbreak,
I'm used to you,
You're all the same,
No matter what I do.

First, you're raw,
An open wound,
Thrown into limbo,
All feelings are doomed.

Next, you're sore,
Time the slow healer,
Recovering from war,
But I still feel her.

Finally, no wait,
My heart will mend,
They'll always be part of them,
Forever until the end.

Unreasonable

There's never a reason,
Real or not,
Nor a chance to alter,
When becoming forgot.

Not a change occurred,
With me at all,
It never does,
But that's my fall.

There's no build-up,
It's not a story,
So sudden it happens,
Lonely becomes mandatory.

Why start,
What you can't finish,
Years wasted swiftly,
To be left diminished.

Safe Mode

My mind ajar,
Flooded with thought,
Lightspeed it travels,
In a position unsought.

All and nothing,
Implosion occurs,
Not through choice,
But neither concurs.

I Shut down,
Mentally so,
The mind is lost,
Damn the memory, though.

Is it safe to start?
With doubts aplenty,
Worked it did,
With a part of me empty.

Your Fault

The fault was on you,
Admitted it you did,
Now I'm without you,
You said little, you hid.

This pain you inflicted,
Avoidable with talk,
It couldn't be predicted,
But you chose to walk.

You say your hearts breaking,
A joke from my perspective,
This is of your making,
I mean look in retrospective.

Forward we go apart,
The future is anew,
Going without my full heart,
Grim, it will be without you.

Theresa May

Theresa may,
You evil witch,
Taking from the poor,
Giving to the rich.

Your party a shamble,
Most are asleep,
The others just ramble,
Shame on your sheep.

Your curtsy a fail,
Dancing more so,
A minister we don't hail,
You've got to go.

The country divided,
Your media is lying,
No help you've provided,
A grim reaper enjoying the dying.

Her

The girl I knew, but a week ago,
Turned from summers warmth to winters snow,
Our being was one, we were complete,
Now torn apart, from veiled deceit.

You were my home, I was no longer a nomad,
Bad words I can't find, to describe what we had,
Alone you've left me, without home or heart,
What we had built, now crumbling apart.

You still have her face, but all else's not there,
Questioning what's real, which parts of you the poseur,
Who I knew is all but gone, no longer a life we share,
The lover becomes a Stanger, a new reality I'm left to bare.

As thoughts fracture, broken as their created,
What does the future hold, for me, the ill-fated?
A reality without you envisioned it was not,
But now all I am to you is a thing to be forgot.

Poison

Love is a poison,
Infecting the mind,
Hearts pump faster,
When two combined.

Given so freely,
Needed by most,
Once it's removed,
Hate's the new host.

Hell are we in,
Or purgatory so,
Pain in plenty,
Hate has new cargo.

It's neither you know,
Perception is key,
Love or hate,
It's all the same to thee.

Feelings

It grows like an oak,
Slowly, with time,
But in an instant,
Cut down, in its prime.

The oak remains still,
For the world to see,
Breaking, withering,
No blossom for thee.

Surrounded by growth,
In the middle of all,
While left lifeless,
Where thou once stood tall.

For years it stays,
Left to be daunted,
It stands no more,
The scene left haunted.

Torn

Memories become broken,
Shattered when they're thought,
A mind self-destructing,
Becomes reset to nought.

New thoughts form,
With pain in their design,
The newly absent haunts them,
My mind is out of line.

Time heals wounds,
That's what the happy say,
Deaf ears thou fall on,
I am but my minds prey.

Synapses overload,
Ripping, breaking and churned,
Recovering through the anguish,
For another lesson learned.

A Brazen Failure

To the time waster,
The stain on my history,
Left suddenly one night,
In an air of mystery.

Another you'd found,
Like a secret, you'd kept it,
A brazen lie used,
For a quick exit.

The shock was caused,
With your gift of despair,
When you left me,
Heartlessly without care.

I did once feel for you,
But no longer I do,
Good luck I wish him,
In putting up with you.

60/40

The mind thinks a lot,
Dying it's thought,
More so than living,
Now harder to thwart.

As time drifts on,
My healing is fading,
It's hurting much harder,
All strengths are jading.

Support all gone,
No lower left to go,
Grim is coming,
Ready to leave, I show.

Going wasn't my choice,
It was vested in thee,
By those who left,
All failed by me.

Where Are You, Me?

I know of my mind,
Every thought, all the care,
But what I don't know,
Is why you're still there?

With a heart broken,
Pieces of you mixed in,
In the space, I'd given you,
For what could have been.

Time heals they exclaim,
But no change I feel,
Days all the same,
Just awake, attempting to deal.

My face paint brave,
All hopes in jest,
Secretly I mourn me,
Questioning, where's my best?

Locked In

I know that I shouldn't,
I don't want it to be,
I am my own prisoner,
Forced living without glee.

Not knowing my sentence,
What for or why so,
A cell of my own creation,
It won't let me go.

I don't want to be here,
Alive without life,
The punishment solitary,
An internal strife.

I fight for a way out,
Blindly severing hurt away,
Attempts mounting the many,
Again, it's not worked today.

When I Wake

When I wake,
My day undecided,
Not bad, nor right,
No thought collided.

If all is well,
The day's a success,
If all is not,
The day turns a mess.

Failure to enjoy,
Results in a fall,
Downward I go,
Unable to stand tall.

If it's the latter,
Happy it be,
These days are rare,
Cherish their glee.

Fight On

I don't want to see you,
Unless in a fire,
Burning you deserve,
A fitting place for a liar.

Deceived, betrayed,
But still, I stand,
Here I am alone,
Through events unplanned.

Dull moments now,
But shine again I will,
In time with progress,
My wounds need to heal.

Better I'll become,
From this lesson taught,
Ready I'll be,
For the next onslaught.

Weekend Break

All the sights to see,
The places to go,
Many miles walked,
You're not here, though.

It's a happy break,
Well, most of the time,
A foreign land it is,
A place without crime.

I think of you,
Although I shouldn't,
Wishing you were here,
I'd hoped I wouldn't.

The trip draws to close,
Many Memories were made,
I lose more thought for you,
With new memories, you fade.

Exposed

You say the words,
That are not true,
Misconceptions,
Of when I was with you.

It took one event,
For me to shine true,
To shatter the lies,
Built by your design.

All I had to do,
Was be my true self,
This was your downfall,
You exposed yourself.

Say no more,
It needn't be said,
The past is the past,
What was had is now dead.

New Year, Just Me

With a date change,
Incessant quotes commence,
New this, new that,
The unknowing, the suspense.

The hope of good,
The unthought-of bad,
Opportunity aplenty,
Experiences to be had.

Why change at all,
Especially for a date,
For if it fails,
You fuel self-hate.

Don't alter at all,
No bettering you need,
Your pace is yours,
Go forth at your speed.

Sleep

I can't find you,
However hard I try,
I need you,
But you're now a lie.

Any time of day,
I use to think of you,
Now I can't function,
I'm owed your time in lieu.

I miss you dearly,
To the point, I'm going insane,
Please come back to me,
It won't be in vain.

We worked so well,
For many times we shared,
Sleeps the name you go by,
Without I've despaired.

Tinderella

In the world of tinder,
All profiles the same,
Loyal, caring, friendly,
Girls gone lost their game.

With professions of a mother,
So many to sift through,
No plans for the future,
Just looking, what about you.

A rare hottie appears,
Right swipe you proceed,
Watch out for them,
They're just after your seed.

No one new around you,
I've completed the dating game,
Not one decent match,
Just those who want insta[2] fame.

---

[2] Insta – Short for Instagram©.

Battle Torn Armour

Credit where credits due,
To all the girls, I'm indebted to you,
For your torment, betrayal, Nastiness to spare,
The pain you inflicted, Without due care.

I write to express,
How you afflicted on me,
Through the wicked acts,
The pain you caused thee.

The hope you removed,
The faith you diminished,
I never gave up,
I'm nearly finished.

My mind now altered,
Armour battle-torn,
Heart in a locked box,
My shell tough and worn.

Battery Symbol

I sit by myself,
Idling on the chair,
Checking my phone,
Let's see who's there.

Insta up to date,
Facebook nothing new,
No recent snaps for me,
Slowly I feel blue.

To thrive off social media,
Hooked I have become,
My thumbs tap constantly,
Addiction I can't escape from.

Phantom vibes occur,
I look down beaming with glee,
It's just the battery symbol,
What a fool I've made of me.

Speed of Thought

Thoughts speed like traffic,
Emotions cloud-like weather,
It's always the same,
Will this be forever.

Nausea kicks in,
Dizzy I'm left,
The road continuous,
To the point of bereft.

A break I need,
A Stop for the traffic,
Noise persists,
The visions are so graphic.

Decelerate the thinking,
Add cover for the weather,
Deal with these metaphors,
I, now, and forever.

Madness

My descent to madness,
I see it coming,
Without confusion,
There's no point running.

Unsure of the real,
The world is blended,
Accelerated thoughts,
Mental wounds are unattended.

Words are normal,
The silence is rotten,
Fear fears itself,
With sanity long forgotten.

The breaks were hit,
They're beyond repair,
All that is left,
Is my soul with a tear.

MC2

Love in my heart,
I feel for thee,
It does not pass,
What's wrong with me.

Days rotate by,
Weeks, months, years,
Thoughts still with me,
To the point of tears.

This is the first love,
Humility was shown,
Weakness brought forth,
But I have humbled alone.

Store dearly I shall,
It pains me to say,
Move on I shalt,
Love will come my way.

Soul State

My struggle with me,
I'm torn between two,
The good and the bad,
When's the latter due?

Happy the hard illusion,
Tiring to brave a face,
While inside I'm crying,
Hiding with grace.

It breaks me to smile,
A false show I put on,
All I want is tears to show,
Break down, run and go.

Even when it happens,
No release I feel,
The soul state I blame,
It's out of time to heal.

It's All So Dark

What is wrong with me,
My mind is not mine,
It's rogue without cause,
I can't recall being fine.

My heart feels alive,
But purposeless so,
Without true love,
I'm filled with sorrow.

Control I am losing,
Desires died and gone,
Death thought a blessing,
This life is done.

Tomorrow still comes,
With all of the above,
Living and dying the same,
I miss my true love.

Carry On

I can be here,
Here is anywhere,
Anywhere but there,
There to bare.

Bare with me now,
Now something new,
New for all,
All of you too.

Too much to be,
Be what you are,
Are you something,
Something at afar.

Far from the rest,
Rest for no one,
One day I'm home,
Home to set the sun.

Solo

What does it mean,
To be alone,
Miles away,
A distance from home.

Is it freedom,
Maybe liberation,
Think more maybe,
Takedown notation.

It's whatever you want,
An escape from the norm,
Growing yourself,
Evolving a new form.

Breaking the comforts,
Threatening the orders,
Down with the patterns,
Expand on your borders.

Poetry Wasn't My Choice

Emotion is the driver,
Taking control of me,
Writing non-stop,
Words are all I see.

I speak to the screen,
With a tip of my finger,
Words are formed,
Until no thoughts linger.

I empty my mind,
For anxiety to subside,
That's not entirely true,
It finds a new place to hide.

Until the next time,
Dormant it lay,
Haunting my mind,
Knowing I'm its prey.

Smokescreen

I think for my life,
My alter ego has a stake,
It controls my being,
I worry I may not wake.

Days of constant battle,
I go to war with myself,
Marginally I win I think,
But what about my health.

I solve problems daily,
But what of my own,
Fixing myself is an issue,
I am helpless and alone.

No one sees these sides,
Dimensions I flow between,
I am in pain and suffering,
How do I remove my smokescreen?

Defeat for Progress

Strength runs low,
The tiring point reached,
Affecting me internally,
Danger inside breached.

The dynamic is you,
A variable I can't omit,
For I must remove it,
To myself, I need to commit.

Harder by day it gets,
Without you and with,
Inside its torment,
Repeatedly I relive.

It rips at me by day,
Awake I lay at night,
This choice not my own,
But through fear of losing the fight.

Sowing the Weight

The weight within me,
Heavier by the hour,
I never saw it coming,
The reason I now cower.

The love I still have for you,
When I know, I should not,
I told myself differently,
But lying caused love to rot.

I need to start fresh,
What's mine is just mine,
No more sharing yours,
Luck will see me fine.

The weight should die with it,
A new beginning, I need,
Planting for my life,
The weight becomes the seed.

Expired Strength

What is it to be strong,
Do we know its end?
What happens then,
Do we break or bend?

Where is its limit,
Do we ever get more?
How does it work,
When strength hits the floor.

Why do we need it?
Does it keep us sane?
Why so does it end,
Making us wane.

For granted, it's taken,
By others as such,
Has there's gone too,
I thought as much.

Alienating Myself

I split in mind, the balance is off,
One side the flame, the other the moth,
All worry suppressed, a deviant free,
Control is lost, I hate you morrow me.

From the highest of high, hitting the low,
Abuse of alcohol or occasional blow,
False freedom I feel, but how long for,
The monsters free and he wants more.

Help! I'm in here, that's not me,
Hacking my life, alienating while free,
The impulse to strong, emotions on a high,
Two sides of my life, but which is the lie.

The morning comes, two days I was out,
I'm back to normal, but heavy with doubt,
I feel its carnage, from the relentless ride,
Back to my Jekyll, escaping my Hyde.

Unfixable

Off the rails, that melted away,
Down the rabbit hole, where a ladder lay,
Off the reservation, no map to return,
These are equivalents to a double U-turn.

I listen to all, absorbing like it's my own,
I become mute, my thoughts are alone,
Plagued with shame, I hush my tongue,
Internalising me, my problems unsung.

The flags are red, but the excitement I see,
Avoid I should but instead help I offer thee,
I drown in emotions that are not mine,
But you're a man, chin up, falsely act fine.

A fix is needed, relentlessly searched for,
I am damaged, repair behind a closed door,
Normal an illusion lost in the dark past,
Future predicts insanity on the forecast.

Empath

To feel what you feel,
A share in your pain,
A mirrored emotion,
Exhaustion to my brain.

Toxicity sensed fully,
Left poisoned I feel,
Avoid all the people,
Unless you can deal.

Thoughts travel at lightspeed,
Confusion to what's mine,
Ours, yours, theirs, hers,
All at the same time.

For years I never knew,
A past full of mood swings,
Is it a blessing or a curse?
Anxiety the future brings.

Anger

The feeling of anger, besieged upon me,
Intense persistence, dark red all I see,
Control is waning, lash out I may,
The toil of this felt, even if I stand or lay.

Unmovable in size, a heavy pressure,
While breaking me, I have no leisure,
Every second thought, anger grows hot,
Rotting inside me, for rest, I cannot.

This anger a gift, from a callous heart,
Given without reason, halting a new start,
To solve I'm hindered, the exit is closed,
To deal I must, with means unknown.

The start it came, from careless betrayal,
Humility the hammer, I was set up to fail,
Vengeance is coming, fuelled by hellfire,
Fear you should, for your outlook, is dire.

A Perfect Night

How hard it is, to feel alone,
Miles away, far from home,
A foreign land, with words of mute,
Clothes unfitting, I had no suit.

This night I say, odd in design,
Laughs with drinks, all is fine,
Dancing with energy, crazy it be,
Then I saw her, and she saw me.

Anke her name, in the centre crowd,
The podium I was, music so loud,
Down I jumped, to her I made way,
A spark was struck, hi I'd say.

Danced we did, genuine with flow,
We had the night, bar to bar we'd go,
The eve's end closes, together we stay,
Until the next time, we get another day.

The Orchestra

My mind is like an orchestra,
Louder and louder it gets,
The noise becomes unbearable,
Deeper and deeper it sets.

No breaks, rhythm or sync,
The tune escaped the sound,
Conductor less I've made myself,
They're nowhere to be found.

This sound sadly heard before,
It's hypnotic by design,
Breaking down evasively,
On the soul, it would dine.

Damaged this will leave me,
The audience, my first thought,
I kept on playing for them,
Just to be left fraught.

Trust

A word with no use,
To all who betray,
Trust me you'd said,
As you fucked it away.

Lies for personal gain,
Dishonesty to save face,
You're less than a human,
A disgrace to the race.

Brazen and conceited,
Entitled with delusion,
Home with other liars,
You deal in their collusion.

Karmas the biggest lie,
A thought for the weak,
It'll never come around,
However hard you seek.

11% Usage

Thinking to dizzy,
A mind overloaded,
I'm not like others,
The basically coded.

Feeling a plants life,
Seeing beyond the real,
Information overload,
Enduring consistently, I deal.

My mind connects,
Without my thought so,
Past, present, future,
A stable flow.

Left to self-regulate,
Beyond a rational realm,
Reality skewed exponentially,
A worn burden is this helm.

Forgetting Myself

To care so much,
But exclude one's self,
It's ill-advised data,
And takes a toll on one's health.

To feel for others,
Their despairing pain,
Purely just to help,
With no personal gain.

Forgetting myself,
Throughout it all,
To be left without,
To feel so small.

Silently screaming,
No sound I exude,
For it's my sanity,
That I alone, exclude.

The Thought Had Crossed My Mind

Finding the words, to describe the pain,
For what I feel, drives me insane,
To attempt I will, to write in rhyme,
The ghost that haunts, my mind this time.

I break in ways, bones could not fathom,
My heart like a fruit, thrown into a chasm,
All thoughts at war, I am ill-prepared,
I fear thy self, for my life I'm scared.

Need not disappear, I'm already alone,
No one else knows for I do not moan,
Unshared this burden, I carry with me,
I tell no one, so they keep their glee.

Even in the end, nothing more feels said,
I still lack the words, you'd hear when I'm dead,
Life just hurts me, it's a lasting kind of pain,
Don't see me as a loss though, for I'm the universes gain.

Checking Myself

Watch something funny, a laugh I'm spared,
What for horror, to make me scared,
Play that song, Goosebumps aplenty,
The main character dies, I don't feel empty.

The safety of bed, but up I wake,
Hunger growls, am I too tired to bake,
Coffee a go-to, water here and there,
Hygiene a given, with logic I care.

To leave the house, with worry I feel,
Small steps but plenty, a daily deal,
Converse with others, the false interest shown,
Reality is dark, it's brighter at home.

The heart still works, broken but beating,
Anxiety struck, with new thoughts fleeting,
Time extends, prolonging this state,
I only wonder how long I must wait.

Painkiller

Painkiller one,
Edge disappears,
Relaxed inside,
Suppressed all fears.

Painkiller two,
Blurred is the mind,
Slurs on all words,
Down I unwind.

Painkiller three,
Staggers in sight,
Movement delayed,
Left feeling delight.

Painkiller four,
Sleep is near,
My body slows,
Shuteye is here.

Humility Birthed Anger

For what I feel, cannot be shown,
No one I trust, I'm here alone,
My thoughts cloud, in a blended mind,
No help from myself, the negatives I find.

I fear my words, on others ears,
It's my burden, I'll deal with the tears,
Past experience, created this pain,
Why O why! Am I put through this again?

Humility I'd shown, a letter was sent,
Deception ensued, down further I went,
It left me with anger, something new for me,
This was the start, now often red, I see.

Can't catch a break, but I'm left broke,
To think on the past, on its toxin I choke,
With the new set up, before our end,
Leaving me nothing, but for my life, I must fend.

Prevalence Revealed

I'm not broken, not any more,
I am healed, but a loss I saw,
My spark is back, with trust removed,
The wall I built for myself improved.

The last trusted, left in the past,
With the heinous act, the darkest cast,
Liberated I am, freedom from others,
Self I look after, my mind unsmothers.

Forward always, with lessons learned,
Fireproof I become, I cannot be burned,
I focus pure sight, my future I build,
I need not no one, I have reskilled.

Untouched I live, with thought as my guide,
Hindsight now dead and new visions applied,
The enemy was me, the devil was in the detail,
No longer emotional, my logic will prevail.

Don't give up.